CORNERSTONES OF FREEDOM™

D0927541

THE SUPREME COURT

BY PETER BENOIT

CHILDREN'S PRESS®
An Imprint of Scholastic Inc.
New York   Toronto   London   Auckland   Sydney
Mexico City   New Delhi   Hong Kong
Danbury, Connecticut

BRINGING HISTORY to LIFE

Content Consultant
James Marten, PhD
Professor and Chair, History Department
Marquette University
Milwaukee, Wisconsin

Library of Congress Cataloging-in-Publication Data
Benoit, Peter, 1955–
  The Supreme Court / by Peter Benoit.
  p. cm. — (Cornerstones of freedom)
  Includes bibliographical references and index.
  ISBN 978-0-531-21332-2 (lib. bdg.) — ISBN 978-0-531-25828-6 (pbk.)
  1. United States. Supreme Court—Juvenile literature. 2. Constitutional his-
tory—United States—Juvenile literature. I. Title.
  KF8742.B435 2014
  347.73'26—dc23   2013026174

All rights reserved. Published in 2014 by Children's Press, an imprint of
Scholastic Inc.
Printed in the United States of America 113

SCHOLASTIC, CHILDREN'S PRESS, CORNERSTONES OF FREEDOM™,
and associated logos are trademarks and/or registered trademarks of
Scholastic Inc.

1 2 3 4 5 6 7 8 9 10 R 23 22 21 20 19 18 17 16 15 14

Photographs ©: Alamy Images: 4 bottom, 18, 56 top (Alliance Images),
36 (Archive Images), 50 (Nick McGowan-Lowe), 16 (ZUMA Press, Inc.);
AP Images: 42, 54 (Charles Dharapak), 29 (John Rous), 55 (Mark Mulville,
The Buffalo News), 11, 12, 14 (North Wind Picture Archives), 7; Corbis
Images: 35, 49 (Bettmann), 41 (Gary Fong/San Francisco Chronicle);
Dreamstime: 51 (Edbockstock), 5 bottom, 23 (Renaschild), 34 (Sixty7a);
Getty Images: 6 (Carl Iwasaki/Time & Life Pictures), 45 (FPG), back cover
(James Brey), 17 (John Moore); Library of Congress: 15, 37; Media Bakery:
4 top, 22 (Hill Street Studios), cover (Tom Brakefield); National Archives
and Records Administration: 27, 44; Newscom/Benjamin E. "Gene" Forte
- CNP: 48; Science Source: 8; Superstock, Inc.: 32 (Everett Collection),
20, 24, 25, 56 bottom, 57; Supreme Court of the United States: 2, 3, 28; The
Granger Collection: 5 top, 10, 13, 26, 30, 33, 38, 47.

Maps by XNR Productions, Inc.

Did you know that studying history can be fun?

BRING HISTORY TO LIFE by becoming a history investigator. Examine the evidence (primary and secondary source materials); cross-examine the people and witnesses. Take a look at what was happening at the time—but be careful! What happened years ago might suddenly become incredibly interesting and change the way you think!

Contents

The Power of the Court

Linda Brown (front, right) attended the segregated Monroe Elementary School before her parents sued the Topeka, Kansas, school board.

Linda Brown could not understand why she was not allowed to attend Sumner Elementary School near her home in Topeka, Kansas. Instead, the third-grader had to walk more than a mile to the all-black Monroe Elementary School. The practice of **segregation**, common at the time, kept black and white students in separate schools. In

THERE HAVE BEEN 112 SUPREME

1951, Linda's father and 13 other parents filed a **lawsuit** in an attempt to end this unfair practice. Three years later, the U.S. Supreme Court decided the *Brown v. Board of Education* case in favor of the families, outlawing school segregation. This decision was a landmark moment in the civil rights movement that changed America forever.

With the ability to make such influential decisions, the Supreme Court wields astonishing power. It has expanded rights for women and minority groups, banned prayer in schools, and limited congressional power. It has even influenced the results of a presidential election. Sometimes its decisions have reflected popular opinion. On other occasions, its decisions have been controversial. Through it all, the court has worked to apply the wisdom of the U.S. Constitution to a world the nation's founders could scarcely have imagined.

In 1954, the Supreme Court was led by chief justice Earl Warren (front row, center).

COURT JUSTICES SINCE 1789.

CHAPTER 1

SHAPING THE LAW

Patrick Henry of Virginia was one of the 56 delegates who made up the Continental Congress.

THE SUPREME COURT WAS

created at a time when things were much different than they are today. The 13 original states were British colonies that united to win independence from Great Britain in the Revolutionary War. Each state was led by a separate **legislature**. Each created its own laws and coined its own money. The states squabbled over lands and had different ideas about how government should be organized. They were held together only weakly by a government known as the Continental Congress. Made up of **delegates** from each state, Congress had some control over military matters and foreign policy, but it could not create national laws to govern the states.

Under the Articles

The Articles of Confederation, **ratified** by all 13 states in 1781, were a small step forward toward a national government. The Articles established a "firm league of friendship" between the states. They also created a very weak central government. Each state had only one vote in Congress, regardless of its population. Congressional committees loosely oversaw laws. However, Congress had no authority to command states. It also could not act directly upon individuals in those states. It had no power to regulate trade between states or collect taxes.

Congress's inability to collect taxes made it difficult to raise the funds needed for its other responsibilities. For example, Congress was in charge of maintaining the nation's army. However, it lacked money to support the troops properly. As a result, the troops lacked supplies and often went months

On December 16, 1777, Virginia became the first state to ratify the Articles of Confederation.

The Battle of Princeton was one of the first American victories of the Revolutionary War.

without pay. When the Revolutionary War ended in 1783, angry soldiers surrounded Congress's meeting place at the Pennsylvania State House to demand payment. They refused to leave for a week.

That protest signaled a larger economic crisis. By 1786, the individual states owed millions of dollars to France, Spain, and the Netherlands. These nations had helped the colonists defeat Great Britain in the Revolutionary War by providing supplies and troops. However, the states had difficulty coming up with the money to repay their allies. For example, Massachusetts taxed its people heavily in an effort to pay its portion of the war debt. Small farmers in the western part of the state were already barely scraping by. They rose in armed protest in an event called Shays's Rebellion.

In January 1787, a man named Daniel Shays led some 1,200 men in an unsuccessful attack on the federal arsenal in Springfield, Massachusetts.

Creating a Constitution

In a panic, Congress called for a Constitutional Convention to be held in Philadelphia, Pennsylvania, the following year. The members of the convention would be responsible for revising the Articles of Confederation to create a stronger national government. Fearing that small states could only lose influence under a strong central government, Rhode Island refused to send delegates. Fifty-five delegates from the remaining 12 colonies met in Philadelphia in May

1787. They did not all agree on how the Articles should be revised. Some wanted to establish a strong union between the states. They pressed for writing a new constitution. Others worried that a strong federal government would have too much power to tax the country's people. They feared that such leadership would be no different than it had been under the rule of Great Britain.

In order to avoid giving too much power to any one state or individual, the delegates decided to spread the responsibilities of the new national government across three branches. The first branch, consisting of Congress, is known as the legislative branch. The Constitution

When the Founding Fathers created the Constitution, they wanted to protect the nation's people from unpleasant events such as when the British government sent its troops to occupy colonists' homes.

George Washington, who had led the American military during the Revolutionary War, played a major role in the Constitutional Convention.

grants this branch the power to create and change the nation's laws. These laws apply to the entire nation, rather than just individual states. This change from the Articles of Confederation finally allowed Congress to collect the taxes it needed to pay for the nation's expenses.

The executive branch of the government is led by the president. The Constitution grants the president the power to either approve or **veto** the laws passed by Congress.

The judicial branch consists of the nation's federal court system. The Constitution grants courts the power to interpret the laws passed by Congress. The courts examine the nation's laws and determine how they apply to specific cases. The Supreme Court lies at the head of this court system.

Checks and Balances

The delegates wanted to ensure that none of the three branches was able to gain too much power over the others. To meet this goal, they wrote into the Constitution a system of checks and balances on the powers of each branch. For example, the president is responsible for nominating federal judges, including Supreme Court justices. However, the president's nominations must be approved by the Senate. This is a check on the president's power.

Additionally, the Senate and the House of

YESTERDAY'S HEADLINES

The Constitution proposed by the delegates in Philadelphia in 1787 needed to be ratified, or approved, by the individual states in order to become law. However, the creation of a powerful central government scared many Americans, especially small farmers. They remembered the abuses of the British government and feared the newly proposed Supreme Court would behave the same.

To help counter these and other fears, delegate Alexander Hamilton (above) wrote a series of essays in support of the new Constitution. One essay promised that the Supreme Court would not be a threat to the people, but a protection against Congress becoming too powerful. The influence of Hamilton's writings helped lead to the ratification of the Constitution.

Representatives must both approve a **bill** for it to pass through Congress. This means the two houses balance out each other's power. The president then has the power to either approve or veto the bill. This acts as a check on Congress's power. Even if the president vetoes a bill, however, Congress can override the veto by securing a two-thirds majority approval in each house. This balances out the president's power over new laws. Later, after the law is put into practice, the judicial branch interprets it and applies it to specific situations. This balances against both the legislative and executive branches.

Members of Congress debate the details of bills before voting whether or not to make them laws.

On September 17, 1787, the delegates signed the completed Constitution and sent it to the states for ratification. Each state carefully studied and debated the document. It took three years, but one by one, all 13 states ratified the new Constitution.

The U.S. Court System

Article III of the U.S. Constitution briefly spells out the basic powers of the Supreme Court. It grants the Supreme Court **jurisdiction** over court disputes between states or between a state and the federal government, and also over cases brought against

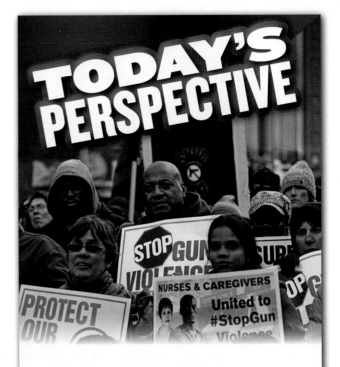

TODAY'S PERSPECTIVE

The Constitutional Convention and the document it created have continued to attract attention for more than two centuries. Opinions about the delegates' true intentions have changed over time. The exact wording of many parts of the Constitution is vague. This leaves some parts open to interpretation. For example, some people believe that the Second **Amendment** to the Constitution guarantees individuals the right to own guns. Others believe that it gives only organized military groups the right to have weapons. It is up to today's courts to decide how the words of the Constitution apply to modern life in the United States.

After helping the United States win the Revolutionary War and helping to shape the Constitution, George Washington was chosen as the nation's first president.

representatives of foreign governments. Article III also establishes the checks and balances on the judicial branch. The Constitution gives Congress the power to establish federal courts beneath the Supreme Court and decide their jurisdiction. Originally, it also granted Congress the right to alter the size of the Supreme Court.

In 1789, Congress determined that one of its first actions would be to create a more detailed plan for the nation's court system. On September 24, 1789, President George Washington signed the Judiciary Act into law. The act specified that the Supreme Court was to consist of six justices. One of them would be designated as the chief justice. Today, there are nine justices on the Supreme Court.

The act divided the nation into judicial districts. A federal court was established in each one. Federal courts are trial courts, and every state has at least one. They hear many types of cases. The vast majority of disputes, however, are heard in state courts. For example, divorces, child custody cases, contract disputes, and most criminal cases are heard in state courts rather than federal courts. As a result, federal courts have limited jurisdiction. They have broad powers within this jurisdiction, however.

The act also granted the Supreme Court the power to hear **appeals** on certain types of lower court decisions. The Supreme Court hears relatively few appeals. Lower courts file appeals when interpretation of federal law is required. Appeals must meet several conditions before the Supreme Court will hear the case. From cases meeting those conditions, the court chooses which ones it will hear based on their relevance to the Constitution. As a result, the Supreme Court has become the ultimate interpreter and protector of the Constitution.

A FIRSTHAND LOOK AT
THE JUDICIARY ACT OF 1789

Article III of the Constitution provided for a Supreme Court, but left the creation of other federal courts to Congress. The Judiciary Act of 1789 spelled out the size and jurisdiction of the Supreme Court. It also created district and circuit courts. See page 60 for a link to read the act online.

CHAPTER 2

DEFENDING
THE CONSTITUTION

Before becoming the first chief justice of the Supreme Court, John Jay was a delegate to the Continental Congress and the chief justice of the New York State Supreme Court.

No one could have guessed that the Supreme Court would one day have as much power as it has today. At the time, George Washington, the nation's first president, struggled to find six men who were willing to serve as justices of the court. The first chief justice, John Jay, stepped down so he could be governor of New York. Other justices grumbled about the travel required of the position, most of it over dangerous roads. Major political figures such as Patrick Henry and Alexander Hamilton simply refused the president's nomination.

Many people believe that elected officials should have more power than Supreme Court justices because they are chosen directly by the country's people.

Concerns About the Court

The Supreme Court's very existence raised concerns among some Americans when it was first established. Critics argued that because Supreme Court justices were appointed instead of elected, they should not have the power to strike down laws created by elected officials. Others wondered how justices—who did not have to answer to voters—could be expected to represent the will of the people. Supporters of the court pointed out that Congress had the power to **impeach** justices who abused their power.

A FIRSTHAND LOOK AT
THE U.S. CONSTITUTION

The Constitution is the document upon which the United States government is based. Though it was written more than two hundred years ago, today's Supreme Court justices still use it as the basis of many of their legal decisions. See page 60 for a link to view the original handwritten Constitution online.

Throughout the court's history, some justices have argued that the court's proper role is not to shape the nation's laws. Other justices believe the court should play a more active role in shaping public policy. As a result, some judges are more willing to overturn existing laws than others are.

The U.S. Supreme Court Building was constructed in Washington, D.C., between 1932 and 1935.

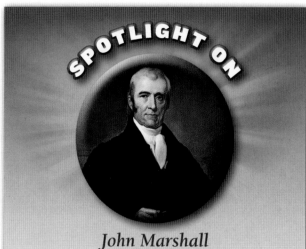

John Marshall

John Marshall served as chief justice of the Supreme Court from 1801 to 1835. During that time, his rulings greatly expanded the power of the court. For example, the court's ruling in *Marbury v. Madison* established judicial review. This power is now viewed as essential to the court's function.

Before he was chief justice, Marshall fought as a soldier in the Revolutionary War. He went on to help ratify the Constitution in Virginia and was later secretary of state. Despite these many accomplishments, he is best remembered for his work on the Supreme Court.

Interpreting the Constitution

President Thomas Jefferson believed that judges should not interpret the Constitution loosely. Loose interpretation might alter understandings of the Constitution or upset the balance of power between federal and state governments by increasing federal powers. Jefferson was often at odds with Chief Justice John Marshall, who favored a broad interpretation of the Constitution.

Marshall reasoned that since the Constitution provided only general guidelines, it invited the court to adapt those guidelines to new challenges.

Under Marshall, the jurisdiction and influence of the Supreme Court was expanded. Before his nomination to the Supreme Court, Marshall had served as secretary of state under President John Adams. Adams had issued several judicial appointments in the closing days of his presidency. Marshall failed to submit the necessary paperwork for the appointments to become official before Adams left office. As a result, James Madison, who was Marshall's successor as secretary of state, was not bound to honor Adams's appointments, and he didn't. William Marbury was one of the men who would have been appointed. He sued Madison to force him to honor the agreement.

The Judiciary Act of 1789 had given the Supreme Court jurisdiction over cases like Marbury's, so it heard the case. However, Marshall declared that the act was unconstitutional, as it had expanded the court's original Article III jurisdiction without amending

James Madison served as secretary of state, and later as the fourth president of the United States.

William Marbury's (above) lawsuit against James Madison led to a ruling that shaped the powers of the Supreme Court.

the Constitution. The Supreme Court ruled against Marbury on the basis that his case was not within its constitutional jurisdiction. In making this ruling, the court granted itself the right to judicial review. Judicial review is the process in which the Supreme Court is able to strike down laws that it deems unconstitutional.

Today, judicial review is central to the function of the Supreme Court. Marshall stated in the ruling for *Marbury v. Madison* that the court's function is "to say what the law is."

Controversy

Sometimes the court's rulings are controversial. In the 2000 presidential election, candidates Al Gore and George W. Bush ran an extremely close race. Bush just barely defeated Gore. However, there was controversy over the way Florida had counted its votes. Because the race was so close, the results in Florida would have been enough to change who won the election. The Florida state government allowed some of the state's nearly six million ballots to be recounted. The recount was nearly a tie. The Supreme Court stepped in. It ruled in *Bush v. Gore* that such

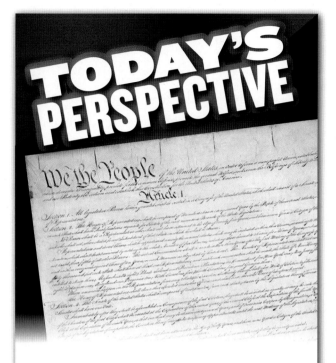

TODAY'S PERSPECTIVE

The power of judicial review is not specifically mentioned in the Constitution. However, the Constitution's creators already seemed to have imagined it before the document had been ratified. Judicial review was established in *Marbury v. Madison*. Later rulings extended that power, allowing the Supreme Court to oversee state courts. Judicial review was controversial. Opponents objected to giving unelected justices the right to overturn congressional legislation. The court continues to be aware of the need to preserve the Constitution while honoring the will of the people.

a recount violated the 14th Amendment. Bush was declared the winner as a result of the decision. After that, many Americans accused the court of unfairly deciding the election.

Choosing the Justices

Justices are chosen not only for their legal abilities, but also because they bring different viewpoints to the court. However, the court has never been a perfect representation of the country's diverse population. For example, only four women have served on the court in its 225-year history. Three of them are serving today. They are Ruth Bader Ginsburg, Elena Kagan, and Sonia

Below are the current justices of the Supreme Court. Front row, left to right: Clarence Thomas, Antonin Scalia, John Roberts, Anthony Kennedy, Ruth Bader Ginsburg. Back row, left to right: Sonia Sotomayor, Stephen Breyer, Samuel Alito, Elena Kagan.

In 1967, Thurgood Marshall became the first black justice to be appointed to the Supreme Court.

Sotomayor. Sotomayor is the first Hispanic justice. Clarence Thomas is the only black justice currently serving, and the second black justice ever. Most justices have followed Protestant religions. However, all nine currently serving are either Jewish or Catholic.

Presidents try to nominate justices from different parts of the country. This way, the differences that exist across the nation may be represented. Justices from different regions bring invaluable diverse experience and diverse views to the court.

CHAPTER 3

CHANGES IN AMERICA

The May 18, 1954, issue of the *New York Times* announced the Supreme Court's decision on *Brown v. Board of Education* on its front page.

The New York Times.

LATE CITY EDITION
Fair and cool today. Mostly sunny, continued cool tomorrow.

"All the News That's Fit to Print"

FIVE CENTS

Copyright, 1954, by The New York Times Company.

NEW YORK, TUESDAY, MAY 18, 1954.

VOL. CIII...No. 35,178.

HIGH COURT BANS SCHOOL SEGREGATION; 9-TO-0 DECISION GRANTS TIME TO COMPLY

McCarthy Hearing Off a Week as Eisenhower Bars Report

SENATOR IS IRATE

President Orders Aides Not to Disclose Details of Top-Level Meeting

President's letter and excerpts from transcript, Pages 24, 25, 26.

By W. H. LAWRENCE
Special to The New York Times
WASHINGTON, May 17 — A secrecy directive by President Eisenhower resulted today in an abrupt recess for at least a week of the Senate's Army-McCarthy hearings.

Democratic and Republican Senators, some publicly and some privately, predicted that the investigation might never resume in earnest. However, there were other Senators who insisted that the investigation would go on to completion.

The recess was voted after Herbert Brownell Jr., the Attorney General, disclosed formally that criminal prosecution might be instituted against those involved in the "preparation and dissemination" of an altered, condensed but still confidential Federal Bureau of Investigation report. This was offered in evidence last week by Senator Joseph R. McCarthy, Republican of Wisconsin.

Republicans outvoted Democrats 4 to 1 on the Senate Permanent Subcommittee of Investigation to recess the hearings until 10 o'clock next Monday morning. They acted amid charges and denials that the way was being prepared for a "white-wash."

Constitutional Division Cited
President Eisenhower cited the constitutional separation of pow-

Communist Arms Unloaded in Guatemala By Vessel From Polish Port, U. S. Learns

State Department Views News Gravely Because of Red Infiltration

Special to The New York Times
WASHINGTON, May 17 — The State Department said today that it had reliable information that "an important shipment of arms" had been sent from Communist-controlled territory to Guatemala.

It said the arms, now being unloaded at Puerto Barrios, Guatemala, had been shipped from Stettin, a former German Baltic seaport, which has been occupied by Communist Poland since World War II. The Guatemalan regime has been frequently accused of being influenced by Communists.

"Because of the origin of these arms, the point of their embarkation, their destination and the

The New York Times May 18 1954
Site of arms arrival (cross)

quantity of arms, involved, the Department of State considers that this is a development of gravity," the announcement said.

A freighter arrived at Puerto

City Colleges' Board Can't Pick Chairman

The Board of Higher Education was unable to elect a chairman at its annual meeting last night at Hunter College.

A spokesman said it was the first time "within memory of board officials" that such a situation had occurred.

Nineteen of the twenty-one members of the board, which governs the four municipal colleges, attended.

Two members nominated for the one-year-term were unable to attain the required majority of eleven votes. They were Joseph B. Cavallaro, who was up for re-election as chairman, and Dr. Harry J. Carman, who was restored to the board on March 2 by Mayor Wagner.

2 TAX PROJECTS DIE IN ESTIMATE BOARD

Beer Levy and More Parking Collections Killed—Payroll Impost Still Weighed

By CHARLES G. BENNETT
Two possible new revenue sources were definitely eliminated yesterday by the Board of Estimate in executive session. They were the proposed 1-cent-a-glass tax on beer and the suggestion to extend metered parking into hours now "free."

In a three-hour City Hall parley the board failed once more

REACTION OF SOUTH

'Breathing Spell' for Adjustment Tempers Region's Feelings

By JOHN N. POPHAM
Special to The New York Times
CHATTANOOGA, Tenn., May 17 — The South's reaction to the Supreme Court's decision outlawing racial segregation in public schools appeared to be tempered considerably today.

The time lag allowed for carrying out the required transitions seemed to be the major factor in that reaction.

Southern leaders of both races in political, educational and community service fields expressed comment that covered a wide range. Some spoke bitter words that verged on defiance. Others ranged from sharp disagreement to predictions of peaceful and successful adjustment in accord with the ruling.

But underneath the surface of much of the comment, it was evident that many Southerners recognized that the decision had laid down the legal principle rejecting segregation in public education facilities.

They also noted that it had left open a challenge to the region to join in working out a program of necessary changes in the present bi-racial school systems.

Three of the most illustrative viewpoints were those expressed by Gov. James F. Byrnes of South Carolina and Herman Talmadge of Georgia, and Harold Fleming, a spokesman for the Southern Regional Council, the most effective interracial organization in the South.

Byrnes Sees Reversal
Governor Byrnes, who has

Associated Press Wirephoto
LEADERS IN SEGREGATION FIGHT: Lawyers who led battle before U. S. Supreme Court for abolition of segregation in public schools congratulate one another as they leave court after announcement of decision. Left to right: George E. C. Hayes, Thurgood Marshall and James M. Nabrit.

1896 RULING UPSET

'Separate but Equal Doctrine Held Out of Place in Education

Text of Supreme Court decree is printed on Page 15.

By LUTHER A. HUSTON
Special to The New York Times
WASHINGTON, May 17 — The Supreme Court unanimously outlawed today racial segregation in public schools.

Chief Justice Earl Warren read two opinions that put the force of unconstitutionality on systems in twenty-one states and the District of Columbia where segregation is permissive or mandatory.

The court, taking cognizance of the problems involved in integration of the schools concerned, put over until the next term, beginning in October, the formulation of decrees to effectuate its 9-to-0 decision.

The opinions set aside the separate but equal" doctrine laid down by the Supreme Court in 1896.

"In the field of public education," Chief Justice Warren said, "the doctrine of 'separate but equal' has no place. Separate educational facilities are inherently unequal."

He stated the court supplied the answer to the question:

"We come then to the question presented: Does segregation of children in public schools solely on the basis of race, even though the physical facilities and other 'tangible' factors may be equal, deprive the children of the minority group of equal educational opportunities? We believe that it does."

MORETTIS' LAWYER MUST BARE TALKS

Jersey Court Orders Counsel to Racketeers in Bergen to Divulge Data to Grand Jury

RULING TO FIGURE IN '54 CAMPAIGN

Decision Tied to Eisenhower —Russell Leads Southerners in Criticism of Court

SOVIET BIDS VIENNA CEASE 'INTRIGUES'

Envoy Warns Austrian Chief on Inciting Soviet Zone— Raab Denies Charges

By JOHN MacCORMAC
Special to The New York Times
VIENNA, May 17 — The Soviet Union warned Austria today to put an end to "hostile and subversive intrigues" against the Soviet occupation forces, or Soviet authorities would do it themselves.

Ivan I. Ilyichev, Soviet High Commissioner, reverted to a prac-

SEVERAL SUPREME COURT rulings have changed the United States in big ways. Some of these landmark cases have changed the way government itself works. Others have addressed issues of racial and social equality. All have reflected back on the words of the Constitution and its authors. These cases highlight the complexity of decisions the Supreme Court makes and their role in shaping the lives of American citizens.

Robert Fulton's first steamship was named the *Clermont*.

Gibbons v. Ogden

The court's 1824 ruling in *Gibbons v. Ogden* has had
far-reaching consequences. In 1807, Robert Fulton and
Robert Livingston built a steamship with two paddle
wheels to travel on the Hudson River in New York. The
success of the new technology soon captured the public
imagination. Fulton and Livingston moved quickly to
dominate the business of Hudson River steam-powered
travel. They even got exclusive rights to the Hudson
from the New York state legislature. Within eight years,
both men had died. Their operation was continued by
a man named Aaron Ogden. A man named Thomas
Gibbons started a rival company.

Ogden claimed that his company had the exclusive
rights to the river that were issued to Fulton and
Livingston. He sued successfully in New York state courts
to force Gibbons out of business. Gibbons argued that

the state's decision violated federal law. He appealed to the Supreme Court. In 1824, the court reversed New York's ruling, citing the "commerce clause" in Article I of the Constitution. This part of the Constitution gives Congress control over commerce that takes place between the states. Commerce usually means financial exchanges between people or organizations. Chief Justice Marshall ruled that commerce included travel. He also ruled that regulating commerce between states gave Congress the

Thomas Gibbons's lawsuit against Aaron Ogden (below) led to a landmark Supreme Court ruling in 1824.

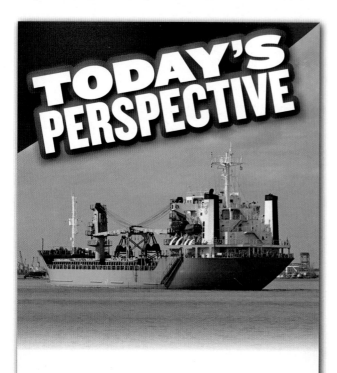

TODAY'S PERSPECTIVE

The Supreme Court's examination of *Gibbons v. Ogden* raised questions of constitutional interpretation. What is commerce? What does "between states" mean? The court established "commerce" as interactions of all types between people, including by way of travel. It also established that commerce within a state could be federally regulated if it influenced interstate commerce.

Critics wonder if the court has used *Gibbons* to weaken state governments. Some believe that the ruling violates the 10th Amendment. This amendment declares that powers not granted to the U.S. government by the Constitution are reserved for state governments. Critics of the Gibbons ruling believe that the court granted the federal government powers that were not outlined in the Constitution.

power to impose laws within a state if it affected interstate commerce. The ruling greatly expanded the reach of the federal government.

The court's ruling encouraged the growth of a national economy. It has also been used to lend support to the Civil Rights Act of 1964. The power of *Gibbons v. Ogden* was repeatedly used in discrimination rulings where a negative influence on interstate commerce could be proved. As a result, hotels, restaurants, and other public places could not discriminate against people of different races. *Gibbons v. Ogden* has also been used

Dred Scott was one of many slaves who attempted to sue for his own freedom prior to the abolition of slavery.

by Congress to create a number of federal criminal laws where the crime negatively affects commerce between states.

Dred Scott v. Sandford

Other landmark rulings reflect the changing attitudes toward race in U.S. society. *Dred Scott v. Sandford* (1857) was meant to resolve a long-standing controversy between free states and slave states. In 1821, Missouri became one of the United States. But Missouri's statehood raised debate on the issue of whether newly admitted states should allow slavery. Congressman Henry Clay proposed the Missouri Compromise. Missouri would be a slave state. States formed in the northern portion of the country would be free of slavery. Those to the south could choose for themselves whether or not to allow slavery.

Years later, Missouri slave owner John Emerson brought an enslaved man named Dred Scott into the Wisconsin Territory, where slavery was banned. Emerson died, leaving his possessions to New Yorker John Sandford. These

Chief Justice Roger B. Taney wrote the most famous part of the Supreme Court's decision on the *Dred Scott* case, declaring that African Americans had "no rights which any white man was bound to respect."

possessions included Dred Scott. Scott sued Sandford in federal court. He claimed that he was free because he lived in a free state. In 1857, the Supreme Court ruled against him. It argued that slaves could never be citizens and that Scott had no right to bring suit in a federal court. It also argued that the Constitution did not give Congress the power to make laws governing slavery. As a result, the Missouri Compromise was deemed unconstitutional. This decision energized the debate over slavery and pushed the nation into the Civil War (1861–1865) a few years later.

At the end of the Civil War, Congress passed the 13th Amendment. It made slavery illegal throughout the nation. However, it did not end discrimination. Congress approved the 14th Amendment in 1868. It extended citizenship and equal protection of the laws to former slaves. That amendment overturned the *Dred Scott* decision.

Plessy v. Ferguson

In the years directly after the Civil War, constitutional amendments gave freed slaves new opportunities for political participation. However, most were still trapped in poverty. Discrimination was widespread. In an 1875 decision, the Supreme Court decided to leave matters of racial segregation

This resolution, signed by Abraham Lincoln and the members of Congress, presented the 13th Amendment to the states for ratification.

to state governments. State and local governments throughout the South enacted laws to keep public facilities segregated. The facilities set aside for black people were usually vastly inferior. Restaurants and restrooms were segregated, as was public transportation. Black people and white people drank from separate water fountains. The segregation of public schools led to long-lasting educational and economic disadvantages for black people.

In 1892, an African American man named Homer Plessy boarded a train car that was for whites only. Plessy was promptly removed from the car and jailed. At trial, Plessy's attorneys argued that the 13th and 14th Amendments had been violated. Judge John Howard Ferguson upheld the

Segregation continued well into the 20th century.

railroad's right to remain segregated as long as it operated within the state of Louisiana. The Louisiana Supreme Court upheld the ruling of the lower court. When an appeal brought the case to the U.S. Supreme Court in 1896, the court upheld the practice of maintaining "separate but equal" facilities for blacks and whites.

Brown v. Board of Education

Discrimination in housing, transportation, jobs, voting, and education continued almost without change for several decades. However, many foreign nations began to look down on the United States for its unfair treatment of black people. Many Americans were also calling for an end to segregation. By the time *Brown v. Board of Education* reached the Supreme Court in 1952, a constitutional crisis was brewing. The justices were deeply divided over whether the 14th Amendment could be interpreted as standing against school segregation. They were also troubled by the idea of overturning a law enacted by Congress several decades earlier. They did not want to intrude on states' rights. Several justices had serious reservations about Brown. However, they recognized that the growing criticism of segregation was a major issue. Justice Earl Warren worked tirelessly to build a **consensus** among his colleagues.

Finally, on May 17, 1954, the court ruled in favor of the students and their families, overturning *Plessy*. All nine of the justices ruled that segregation in public schools violated the 14th Amendment.

Korematsu v. United States

On December 7, 1941, Japanese forces launched a surprise attack on the U.S. Naval Base at Pearl Harbor, Hawaii. The attack raised concerns that Japanese Americans might pose a threat to national security. As a reaction to this fear, the U.S. government ordered that Japanese Americans be rounded up and placed in camps. More than 100,000 people were forced to sell their possessions and give up their jobs in order to move into these camps.

Instead of giving in to this harsh treatment, Japanese American Fred Korematsu decided to stay in his home. He was arrested for his decision, and his case reached the Supreme Court on appeal. In a 6-3 decision,

A FIRSTHAND LOOK AT
KOREMATSU V. UNITED STATES

The Supreme Court's ruling in *Korematsu v. United States* remains controversial even today. In the early 2000s, it was used to expand the government's powers during President George W. Bush's war on terror. See page 60 to read the *Korematsu* ruling online.

the court ruled against Korematsu. It stated that the movement of Japanese Americans into camps was not based on race, but simply a matter of national security. The ruling also states that "hardships are part of war." The court's ruling in *Korematsu v. United States* divided the nation. However, its decision was never overturned.

In 1998, Fred Korematsu was awarded the Presidential Medal of Freedom for his efforts to resist the poor treatment of Japanese Americans during World War II.

CHAPTER 4

THE SUPREME COURT AND YOUR RIGHTS

Antonin Scalia (left) is the longest-serving justice currently on the Supreme Court. He was appointed in 1986 by President Ronald Reagan.

IN ADDITION TO OUTLINING the structure of the U.S. government, the Constitution and its amendments lay out the personal freedoms that are granted to U.S. citizens. As interpreters of the Constitution, the justices of the Supreme Court have helped shape the details of these rights. Throughout history, new situations have arisen that change the way we think about our rights. In these cases, it has been up to the Supreme Court to decide how the Constitution applies to modern life.

The Debate Over Free Speech

No right is as highly prized or debated as the freedom of self-expression. Though the First Amendment protects free speech, there are exceptions. For example, speech must not violate standards of common decency. The amendment also does not protect defamation. Defamation is when someone spreads lies to intentionally harm another person's reputation. Similarly, the First Amendment does not protect "fighting words" that are likely to provoke a violent response.

The First Amendment also prohibits speech that encourages specific illegal actions. The Supreme Court's rulings have continued to define standards for acceptable speech. During World War I (1914–1918),

Many people have strong opinions about the interpretation of the amendments in the Bill of Rights.

The Alien Registration Act made it illegal to promote violent overthrow of the government or to belong to a group that promoted such things. This law was used to place Communist Party leaders such as Gus Hall (left), Henry Winston (center), and John Gates (right) on trial.

a man named Charles Schenck distributed pamphlets encouraging resistance to the military **draft**. The court ruled that Schenck's actions were a "clear and present danger" to the United States in wartime.

The debate on free speech took yet another turn in the 1950s. The Alien Registration Act was passed by Congress in 1940. It was intended to bar Communist Party membership in the United States. Communists promoted violent overthrow of the U.S. government. However, many people saw the act as a violation of their right to express political beliefs. In a 1951 ruling, the Supreme Court upheld the Alien Registration Act. By 1957, the court had changed its position. It ruled in *Yates v. United States* that the First Amendment did not protect speech calling for specific violent action. However, speech in support of Communist beliefs was protected.

Similarly, the court ruled in *Brandenburg v. Ohio* in 1969 that the hate group known as the Ku Klux Klan could hold rallies calling for violent opposition to civil rights laws. However, it could not ask demonstrators to engage in violence at a specific place and time.

It has been up to the Supreme Court to decide whether or not hurtful or hateful forms of self-expression are protected by the First Amendment. In 1992, the Supreme Court struck down a law in St. Paul, Minnesota. The law banned the display of symbols likely to arouse anger toward others based on race, religion, and other factors. The court ruled that the use of these symbols was protected by the First Amendment.

Speaking Out at School

Limiting free speech appropriately is even more difficult in schools. Students' free speech rights are protected by the First Amendment. However, schools must also be kept free of distractions so students can learn. In 1965, John and Mary Beth Tinker wore black armbands to their high school to protest the Vietnam War. Both were suspended. In 1968 and 1969, the Supreme Court heard *Tinker v. Des Moines Independent Community School District*. In a landmark ruling, Justice Abe Fortas wrote the court's opinion. Fortas noted that the armbands were a silent

Mary Beth and John Tinker were just 13 and 15 years old, respectively, when they became part of the landmark Supreme Court case that reinforced students' right to free speech.

protest that did not interfere with order or discipline in the school. Students, he continued, "are possessed of fundamental rights which the State must respect."

A FIRSTHAND LOOK AT
TINKER V. DES MOINES INDEPENDENT COMMUNITY SCHOOL DISTRICT

Tinker was a landmark ruling in the ongoing discussion of "school speech." It helped to establish the principle that self-expression that did not promote classroom disruption would be constitutionally protected. See page 60 to read the court's ruling online.

Justice Byron White was a professional football player in the NFL before serving on the Supreme Court.

In other rulings, the court has sided with school districts wanting to limit crude language, agreeing that it is "inconsistent with the fundamental values of public school education." In one decision, *Bethel School District v. Fraser* (1986), Justice Byron White stated that students in public schools did not have the same rights of free expression as adults outside the school did. In *Hazelwood School District v. Kuhlmeier* (1988), the court went farther in protecting the interests of schools. Its decision supported schools' rights to regulate the content of school-sponsored newspapers.

In later decisions, the court continued to grant school administrators control over student self-expression at school-sponsored events. In *Morse v. Frederick* (2007), the court upheld an Alaskan school's disciplinary action of a student who had displayed a banner that seemingly promoted illegal drug use. However, the court was deeply divided over the case. Justice John

Paul Stevens argued that no evidence had been provided that the banner would increase drug use. He believed that the ruling was a violation of the student's right to self-expression.

Privacy Rights

The Supreme Court has also placed limits on students' privacy rights in school. A 1985 ruling, *New Jersey v. T.L.O.*, supported a school's right to search student lockers and backpacks if faculty members suspect a crime has been committed. A 1995 case confirmed a school's right to require drug tests for athletes. In 2002, the

TODAY'S PERSPECTIVE

The Supreme Court's 1988 ruling in *Hazelwood v. Kuhlmeier* established a school's right to regulate student self-expression. Since *Hazelwood*, the court has continued to support schools over the individual freedoms of students. Critics of the ruling point out that it limits the protection of free speech for students. They argue freedom of the press guarantees that government cannot censor printed material before it is published. However, school administrators such as Hazelwood East High School principal Robert Reynolds (above), whose actions led to *Hazelwood v. Kuhlmeier*, censor in exactly this way. Critics argue that this has a worrisome effect on the freedom of expression.

A police officer rubs a cotton swab on the inside of a suspect's mouth to collect a DNA sample.

court reviewed *Board of Education v. Earls*. Once again, the court sided with school districts by supporting a school's right to require drug tests for all students participating in extracurricular activities.

Students aren't the only ones who are experiencing challenges to traditional ideas about privacy rights. In reviewing *Maryland v. King* (2013), the Supreme Court supported the right of police officers to collect DNA samples from individuals arrested for a crime. The samples could be placed in a national database. Many people see this as an invasion of privacy.

Other Supreme Court decisions are in support of stronger privacy rights. In *United States v. Jones* (2012), the court ruled that police officers could not place a tracking device on a suspect's car without a **warrant**. The decision was a major victory for the rights protected by the Fourth Amendment.

Many Americans are concerned that law enforcement agencies are using state-of-the-art technology to monitor law-abiding citizens. They worry that laws passed in response to the war on drugs and the struggle against terrorism have empowered law enforcement to pry into people's private lives. These and other matters will eventually be settled by the Supreme Court. The court will look to the Constitution for guidance in an ever-changing world. It will work to strike a proper balance between protecting the rights of Americans today while being true to the vision of the Founding Fathers.

Technology and Privacy Issues

As technology changes the way people share information, many Americans are concerned about the way it will affect their privacy rights. The Fourth Amendment guarantees citizens a reasonable expectation of privacy. However, conducting everyday business over the Internet usually requires that citizens share personal information with banks, privately owned businesses, and others. Government and law enforcement agencies can access and search this information without a warrant. Many Americans fear that this increases the likelihood of law enforcement abusing its power.

What Happened Where?

OREGON

IDAHO

MONT

NORTH DAKOTA

SOUTH DAKOTA

WYOMING

NEVADA

UTAH

COLORADO

NEBRASKA

KANSAS

Topeka, KS
The landmark *Brown v. Board of Education* case, which legally ended school segregation, began in Topeka when Linda Brown's parents sued to win her the right to attend an all-white school.

ARIZONA

NEW MEXICO

OKLAHOM

Juneau, AK
In the 2007 *Morse v. Frederick* case, the Supreme Court upheld the decision of a Juneau high school to limit its students' freedom of speech.

TEXAS

ALASKA

Juneau ●

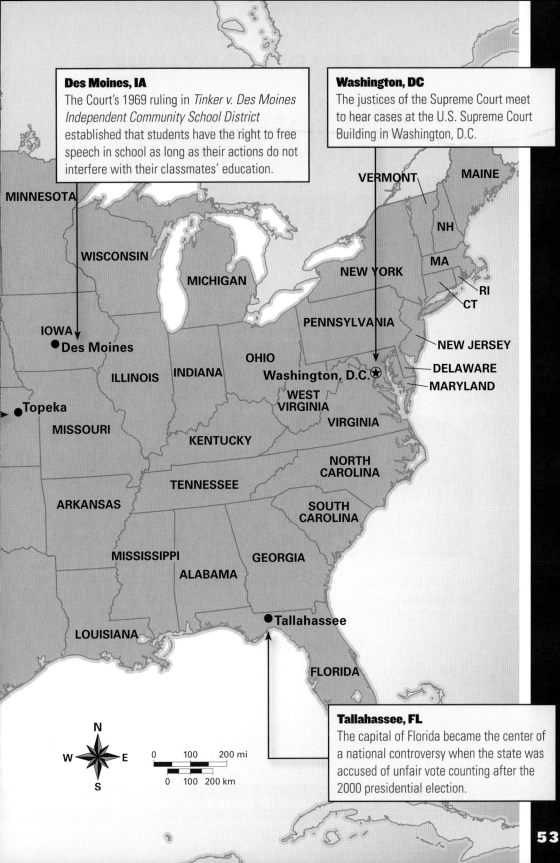

Des Moines, IA
The Court's 1969 ruling in *Tinker v. Des Moines Independent Community School District* established that students have the right to free speech in school as long as their actions do not interfere with their classmates' education.

Washington, DC
The justices of the Supreme Court meet to hear cases at the U.S. Supreme Court Building in Washington, D.C.

Tallahassee, FL
The capital of Florida became the center of a national controversy when the state was accused of unfair vote counting after the 2000 presidential election.

MINNESOTA

WISCONSIN

MICHIGAN

VERMONT

MAINE

NH

NEW YORK

MA

RI

CT

PENNSYLVANIA

IOWA

Des Moines

OHIO

INDIANA

Washington, D.C.

NEW JERSEY

DELAWARE

MARYLAND

ILLINOIS

WEST VIRGINIA

Topeka

MISSOURI

KENTUCKY

VIRGINIA

NORTH CAROLINA

TENNESSEE

ARKANSAS

SOUTH CAROLINA

MISSISSIPPI

GEORGIA

ALABAMA

Tallahassee

LOUISIANA

FLORIDA

N
W E
S

0   100   200 mi

0   100   200 km

Unforeseen Circumstances

Justice Elena Kagan was appointed to the Supreme Court in 2010 by President Barack Obama.

From its humble beginnings, the Supreme Court has grown in power and status. Its rulings have driven the growth of federal power and changed the understanding of the Constitution in ways its creators could not have foreseen. To best serve the public will, the court must continue to respect the voices of ordinary citizens and their understanding of the Constitution.

That challenge is a formidable one. The pace of social and technological change has never been greater. Technological advances have increased personal freedom but threatened privacy. Terrorism has disturbed the delicate balance between privacy and safety. If we are to continue to enjoy the freedoms granted by the Constitution, we must look to the wisdom of the Supreme Court.

John Roberts is the 17th chief justice of the United States.

SERVING SUPREME COURT JUSTICE EVER.

INFLUENTIAL INDIVIDUALS

George Washington

George Washington (1732–1799) was a Revolutionary War general who was named president of the 1787 Constitutional Convention. Later, he served as the first president of the United States.

Thomas Jefferson (1743–1826) was the chief author of the Declaration of Independence. He later served as the first U.S. secretary of state, second U.S. vice president, and third U.S. president.

John Jay (1745–1829) was the first chief justice of the United States. He resigned his position in order to become governor of New York.

Alexander Hamilton (1755–1804) was a delegate to the Constitutional Convention. His writings in support of the Supreme Court helped convince the nation that its inclusion in the Constitution was a good idea.

John Jay

John Marshall (1755–1835) was the fourth chief justice of the United States. He decided many important cases and is known as one of the most influential justices in the history of the court.

Dred Scott (ca. 1795–1858) was a slave who sued for his freedom. The Supreme Court ruled against him in a landmark 1857 decision.

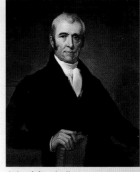
John Marshall

Earl Warren (1891–1974) was the chief justice who helped build a consensus in the Supreme Court against school segregation in *Brown v. Board of Education* (1954).

Fred Korematsu (1919–2005) fought against the U.S. government's policy of placing Japanese Americans in internment camps during World War II. The Supreme Court decided against him in a landmark 1944 case.

1781

The Articles of Confederation are ratified.

1787

The Constitutional Convention is held in Philadelphia, Pennsylvania.

1824

Gibbons v. Ogden establishes Congress's right to regulate interstate commerce.

1857

Dred Scott v. Sandford upholds slavery.

1896

Plessy v. Ferguson upholds the policy of "separate but equal" public facilities for black and white Americans.

1954

Brown v. Board of Education strikes down the *Plessy v. Ferguson* decision.

1969

Tinker v. Des Moines Independent Community School District grants students the right to free speech at school.

1789

The Judiciary Act creates federal courts.

1801–1835

John Marshall serves as chief justice.

1803

Marbury v. Madison greatly expands the court's powers of judicial review.

1919

Schenck v. United States establishes "clear and present danger" policy.

1944

The Supreme Court issues its decision on *Korematsu v. United State*s.

2000

Bush v. Gore settles a close presidential election.

2007

In *Morse v. Frederick*, the Supreme Court sides with schools in regulating student self-expression at school events.

2013

In *Maryland v. King*, the Supreme Court supports the right of police officers to collect DNA samples from crime suspects.

LIVING HISTORY

Primary sources provide firsthand evidence about a topic. Witnesses to a historical event create primary sources. They include autobiographies, newspaper reports of the time, oral histories, photographs, and memoirs. A secondary source analyzes primary sources, and is one step or more removed from the event. Secondary sources include textbooks, encyclopedias, and commentaries. To view the following primary and secondary sources, go to www.factsfornow .scholastic.com. Enter the keywords **Supreme Court** and look for the Living History logo Σ᠂.

The Judiciary Act of 1789 The Judiciary Act of 1789 expanded upon Article III of the U.S. Constitution by outlining the size and jurisdiction of the Supreme Court. It also created district and circuit courts.

Korematsu v. United States During World War II, the United States government forced Japanese Americans to give up their homes and jobs and live in poor conditions in internment camps. Japanese American Fred Korematsu resisted this practice, and his case went all the way to the Supreme Court.

Tinker v. Des Moines Independent Community School District *Tinker v. Des Moines* was a landmark ruling concerning the degree of free speech granted to students. It helped establish the idea that students had the right to freely express themselves in school as long as their actions did not interfere with the education of their classmates.

The U.S. Constitution The Constitution is the main outline of the United States government. Despite its age, the Constitution remains the cornerstone of U.S. law, and the Supreme Court continues to rely on the document for guidance in its decisions.

RESOURCES

Books

Benoit, Peter. *Brown v. Board of Education*. New York: Children's Press, 2012.

Burgan, Michael. *The U.S. Constitution*. New York: Children's Press, 2012.

Gold, Susan Dudley. *Tinker v. Des Moines: Free Speech for Students*. Tarrytown, NY: Marshall Cavendish Benchmark, 2007.

Raatma, Lucia. *The Bill of Rights*. New York: Children's Press, 2012.

Visit this Scholastic Web site for more information on the Supreme Court:
www.factsfornow.scholastic.com
Enter the keywords Supreme Court

GLOSSARY

amendment (uh-MEND-muhnt) a change made to a law or legal document

appeals (uh-PEELZ) applications to a higher court for a change in a legal decision

bill (BIL) a written plan for a new law

consensus (kuhn-SEN-sus) an agreement among all the people in a discussion or meeting

delegates (DEL-i-gits) people who represent a larger group of people at a meeting

draft (DRAFT) a system that required young men in the United States to serve in the armed forces

impeach (im-PEECH) to bring formal charges against a public official for misconduct

jurisdiction (jur-is-DIK-shuhn) the power of a court or other authority to make and enforce legal decisions

lawsuit (LAW-soot) a legal action or case brought against a person or a group in a court of law

legislature (LEJ-iss-lay-chur) the part of government that is responsible for making and changing laws

ratified (RAT-uh-fyed) agreed to or approved officially

segregation (seg-ruh-GAY-shuhn) the act of separating people based on race, gender, or other factors

veto (VEE-toh) to stop a bill from becoming a law

warrant (WOR-uhnt) an official document that gives permission for something, such as searching or arresting someone

INDEX

Page numbers in *italics* indicate illustrations.

ABOUT THE AUTHOR

Peter Benoit is the author of dozens of books for Children's Press. He has written about American history, ancient civilizations, ecosystems, and more. He is also a historical reenactor, occasional tutor, and poet. He has written more than 2,000 poems. Peter is a graduate of Skidmore College, with a degree in mathematics. He lives in Greenwich, New York.